I0777080

**In Defence of "Sexism":
Confessions of a Convicted Masculinist**

By Elias Lundgren
Translated from the Swedish by Peter Falkstein

For Georg, my son
(and only mine).

May Odin give you knowledge on your path,
May Thor grant you strength and courage on your way,
And may Loki give you laughter as you go.
– Traditional Viking blessing

I am Elias Lundgren. I am 34 years old. I am a man. I have balls. Do any of these facts make me a criminal?

Of course they do.

Having balls makes me a "sexist".

Having balls makes me a liar and a cheat.

Having balls makes me an unspeakably privileged embodiment of inequality. It makes me a bully, a beater of women, and a rapist.

Doesn't it?

One thing I am most certainly not – I am not an 'Egalitarian' or anything close. The idea of complete equality between the genders is, without question, the most pernicious and dangerous ideology to emerge from the 20th century. Gender equality is not only undesireable – if it were ever implemented, it would spell the end of democratic civilisation.

In this book I will draw on my own expertise as an amateur professor of Gender Studies, as well as a lifetime of careful attention devoted to economics and sociology, to present the definitive counterargument to the so-called 'equality' agenda.

A necessary disclaimer – no misogynists allowed beyond this point. I do not hate women; in fact, I love them more than life itself. However, I'm sorry girls, but like many other perfectly decent and virile men I also happen to love democracy and civilisation.

We have spent our lives being told that everything relevant to the gender equality debate had already been said.

We were told that women must have the first, last, and only word on feminism. We were told wrong. In reality, woman has used her influence to force man to bite his tongue, and leave unsaid many things which must be said. In this book, I will attempt to repel that influence, and I will attempt to say those things.

My name is Elias Lundgren. I have balls. I am not ashamed.

The first step: legalising logic

Before we begin our analysis properly, permit me a moment to lay down some ground rules. Women have restricted all logical discussion on gender equality by two main methods, which have to be dispensed with before we can really have a rational conversation about these issues.

First and foremost, with the aid of the liberal media, women have essentially outlawed logic.

By this I mean that they have successfully forbidden men from generalising in any way about women. They justify this ban by three main appeals to "reason": first, they tell us that any generalised assessment will not apply to every woman; second, that generalisations as a rule are not practically applicable; and third that the scientifically verified differences between men and woman, physically, cannot in any way impact the roles women can play in society.

They have gone further than this however, outlawing any man who dares to utter any 'hurtful' or 'offensive' sentiments about women publicly. It should go without saying that, in the course of any serious scientific discussion, avoiding 'hurt feelings' cannot be the utmost, inviolable standard. Did Charles Darwin worry about the 'hurt feelings' of his readership of religious zealots and Victorian perverts? Did Einstein worry about 'hurting the feelings' of those who didn't understand his ideas about relativity and light-speed?

I must demand that anyone reading this book follows the example of the man who wrote it, and sets aside those arbitrary feminist 'laws' for the purposes of rational discussion. Socially, I am as chivalrous as the next man – even my ex-wife would have attested to that – but a nation cannot declare war on another, then expect to be treated with full diplomatic niceties.

Make no mistake, men. We are at war.

Firstly, in connection with this futile ban on all generalisation, can we please just take a deep breath and register logically that all generalisations – not only those which relate to women – are subject to exceptions? The idea that because there are exceptions there can be no validity to generalisation itself is ludicrous. In fact the exception often proves the rule, as they say.

"Most swans are white" is a generalisation. Does that necessarily make it false? If someone runs up to me clutching a black swan in her arms, crying "I found a black swan! Elias was wrong!" –– does that prove, *a priori*, that most swans are black? Of course it doesn't. The black swan is an aberration; an exception that proves the rule. Despite the existence of exceptions, the generalisation in this case represents an unimpeachable example of 'deductive logic'.

Furthermore, let us also make clear to ourselves that virtually all decisions made in the course of the average man's life, as well as all decisions made by judges in legal cases, are to some extent founded on generalisation. The question of feminism, and with it the larger question of the proper role women should take in society, can only be solved by appealing to generalisation – as to what imprint the physical female sex leaves on a woman's physical abilities, as to a woman's character, and as to a woman's intellect. The 'secondary' sexual characteristics of woman are not really at all secondary when it comes to the issue of gender equality! Rather than generalisation being the enemy of reason in this case, it is a vital tool in determining the proper place of each gender. It's only by a careful application of rational, logical generalisations that we can we arrive at answers to the questions at hand.

When it comes to the absurd idea that we should be careful not to say anything which could be deemed 'offensive' or 'hurtful' to women, even if it is logically correct, well... Ladies of a nervous disposition, cover your ears while this crude, sexist barbican humbly points out that, while it made perfect sense to avoid speaking ill of women when they kept to an idyllic life of quiet domestic bliss, now that women insist on insinuating themselves into the wider world of discourse, it is quite fair that they should lose the privileged and protected position which went hand in hand with their silence.

There is no sacred circle drawn around you, ladies, forbidding the entrance of logic or of counter-argument into your perfumed atmosphere. I am sorry. There is no magic pixie dust which will help you to hover above the ground, no matter how many happy thoughts you cling to. I am so, so sorry. You wanted to break into the real world – well, here it is.

The next most important thing to determine is the pact between myself and yourself, dear reader. These discussions are rightfully controversial, and it's important that a bond of trust between author and disciple be firmly established if any progress is to be made.

Before any useful discourse can be engaged in, it's vitally important that an agreement should be reached as to what kind of discourse will carry what level of authority, what the foundations will be of our main logical terms. In a sense we need to 'beat the bounds' of our argument, and determine where the goalposts will be for the duration of the 'match'. I can achieve this by illuminating the philosophy of logic which I will hold myself to throughout the book.

I do not claim for myself any kind of 'dogmatic' or automatic authority. If there's one thing prison teaches a man, it's humility. Yesterday I had to beg another man for toilet paper to wipe the shit out of my arsehole – that, my friends, is an express lane highway to humility. Still, I will be using some of the literary structures associated with dogmatic argument, out of necessity. This is a subtle, but important distinction.

I would never accept the designation as some kind of inspired 'guru' figure, even if it were thrust upon me. After 15 years of marriage, I know all too well the resentment which festers in the heart of a supplicant who worships her husband (or author) as a living god. If the sole basis for my arguments is my own status as an authority figure, anyone will be able to dismiss them simply by attacking me personally.

I have no intention of claiming that kind of automatic right to respect and credibility. Neither am I so arrogant as to insist that the pages of this book contain absolute proof of the argument I am proposing. This book only represents a 'thesis' or 'theory' – one which, I believe, is being proven and re-proven over and over again in the world at large.

The kind of proof which can be sought when it comes to factual matters is not possible when one speaks of a more general or larger 'truth' of the world. Absolute proof is the province of mathematicians, geneticists, neuroscientists and eugenicists.

In all else, the best we can do is look for principles which are, to a greater or lesser degree, 'probable' – not 'provable'. This means there is always some insecurity in the conclusions which we arrive at. It is obvious that in sociology, in political economy, literary criticism, philosophy etc.., we are always dealing with propositions dressed up as certainties, rather than certainty itself.

In time of war it may be necessary for a general or captain to treat his troops as if he himself is a King, and they his subjects, out of sheer pragmatism and the need for decisive action. However, when all's said and done, the general and his troops both know that he is no King; and when they follow his orders it is not through belief that he possesses some sort of divine right, but simply out of that same spirit of pragmatism.

I will set before you definitions and generalisations on this subject as and when they recommend themselves to my reason, always on the understanding that they must then be subject to your own judgment. I set them before you as the end result of long and dedicated efforts to recall and analyze the whole of my life experience on women and gender equality, and to hypothesise as to the common elements uniting my experiences with those of other men.

No attempt will be made at a generalisation about women as a sex, until I have endeavoured to recall without prejudice all the many individual women I have known, and to elucidate from my experiences with them the characteristics common to all – leaving out only (except when they are my specific focus) all outwardly deviant specimens.

My little sister was retarded. Sorry SJWs, that is not a term of abuse – it is a literal descriptor. My retard sister suffered from cerebral palsy, and I took care of her every day of my life from the time I was old enough to walk. I loved her, and cared for her, and watched her back, carried her up and down stairs when she was too tired to lift her legs. When other kids called her names, I beat them until my fists were bloody and bruised. When that happened, my sister would bind them for me while she sang her own strange, broken songs to comfort me.

My retard sister was the best and kindest female I have ever known – but she was in no way a normal, functional representative of her sex. It would be quite wrong to include her in my overall assessment in this book, which will be concerned only with the wider, mainstream traits of womankind, rather than individual outliers.

If it should happen that you, kind reader, agree with any of my generalisations, that particular hypothesis will naturally no longer be the opinion of one man. His agreement will reinforce and raise it up in stature as an intellectual accord between two distinct minds. This is how we build the links in our chain.

If, however, some reader should conclude that one of my generalisations is out of line with her own opinions (which are, of course, far superior!), that generalisation will be held down and castrated as she demands, stripped of its pride and authority to satisfy her shrill demands.

In either case, of course, no one mind has absolute authority, and each generalisation must be examined by as many pairs of eyes as possible. This approach, like all logical systems of though, is basically Darwinian – each idea when first conceived will be tested. Depending on its level of strength or weakness, it will be accepted and be endorsed as truth; or it will be be recognised as false, and find its place with the other runts and rejects of evolution, which will inevitably be culled and crushed under the wheels of progress.

Even as I type these words, I can hear a high-pitched, repetitive voice – let us be clear, a *female* voice – nagging me constantly. It is the voice of my ex-wife, I know it, telling me not to continue. Telling me that I must not say such horrid things. Telling me that generalisation from personal experience is not a valid form of argument; that just because an idea persists in common thought, it is not necessarily correct.

I will say to the voice now what I said the last time I heard it – telling me that I have run Georg's bath too hot, again.

Shut up and leave the room, you sallow, broken-down old mule.

PART I – The Enemy

1. Women afflicted by feminism (and the "men" they infect)

The task I must first take is to show that the feminist movement has no real intellectual or moral sanction and that there are very important reasons why the fundamental principles of feminism are not surrendered to by men. First, I want to analyze the mental attitude of those who are on the side of feminism and then continue the main arguments on which feminism is based.

The majority of women who support feminism do not do it on reasons of public interest or philanthropy. They are almost entirely influenced by two motives: outrage by the suggestion that a woman must inherently be subordinate to the behavior and wishes of men; and the rejection of a society in which more money, more personal freedom (in fact, more of the personal freedom that gives one money), is becoming more and more publicly recognized as the just property of man.

A cause which is tied so feebly to charitable concerns and public interest and has such a dependence on emotional inflammation and delusions of grandeur does not actually have any moral status. For its intellectual status, the feminist movement almost entirely depends on the fact that it has the advocacy of a number of mighty men. It will be necessary to examine these men and their advocacy.

The "intellectual" male who seems to be the name associated with feminist causes and articles will often, when you press him, make this confession. "Feminism," he says, "is a serious and important issue, but the fiery female feminist will not achieve what she thinks she is going to, but will leave things exactly as they are. However, providing full gender equality to women is desirable from the point of view of justice, and it will soothe the tempers of a large number of very worthy women".

It can be defined as the broadly general rule that only two classes of men really serve the cause of feminism. The first is a social justice warrior who, when he considers that he has taken on a moral principle, immediately enters the fight without engaging his logical faculties at all.

The other is that very strange type of man who, when you say during an audience with him that a particular woman should be measured by certain intellectual and moral standards as inferior to the average human being, he solemnly and almost tearfully asks: "Do you know, sir, that you are insulting my wife?".

For this kind of man, any unfavorable criticism of a woman is a personal insult to himself. We find him on his wedding day, in a state of indignation with UK marriage laws; he righteously gives up any authority over his bride, and promises her all protections against any violations of her freedom that may proceed.

This woman he will always credit for his own intellectual achievements. He sees woman and all her works through detached retinas – detached, that is, from a working brain! It is incomprehensible to him that there might be any opposition to the sexes working equally side by side in any given workplace. He cannot acknowledge that the physical differences between genders in these circumstances penetrate and undermine parts of society that would be best unencumbered by this confusion.

However, this infidelity to the facts on his part cannot consist only of constitutional defects in his vision. When dealing with women, the mind and the moral sense of this man are no longer his own. We begin to have our suspicions of his moral sincerity when we find him insisting zealously that woman's behavior to man is always morally unimpeachable. For no sincere mind can allow, for example, that a woman who lives in a state of financial dependence on a man can morally claim unrestricted freedom.

Allow your humble author a little trip down memory lane. It is Autumn. My (now ex) wife and I have, at the time, been married for a little over five months. Sidling up to me in the kitchen, she begins to keen "Eliaaas, we need a new washing machiiiiine! Can you debit the money to my account!"

But honey, I reply, the washing machine works fine. Why do we need a new one?

"This one looks so old and grubbyyyyy," she says, cooing and pouting like a little girl because she knows what that does to a man. "Don't I deserve a nice shiny neeeew one!".

Laughing indulgently, I decide to respond to her schoolgirl routine, leaning in manfully and taking hold of her soft yet shapely buttock. "Don't worry little girl," I growl; "you just let Daddy take care of everything".

She steps back with real venom in her eyes; a look of true disgust. "Don't talk to me like that Elias, you know I hate it". With that, she turns and leaves the room.

That night, of course, we fuck like wild gorillas in the jungle.

What lessons should poor, unsuspecting Young Elias have learned from this experience? First and foremost, that every true woman is a natural expert at walking the tightrope of hypocrisy between submitting to a man's financial dominance, and demanding that he play along with her delusions of independence.

Our suspicion of dishonesty or self-deception in a man who plays along with these strategies is confirmed by further attention to his arguments. They are often filled with fake analysis, misplaced or mixed metaphors, or arguments used to paper over some weakness in the feminist case. It is a special trait of these men to state their intention to tackle concrete problems, and then spend all their time and energy on abstractions.

Rather than engaging with flesh and blood women in an existing environment of real conditions, this man always argues in the name of a woman who is a creature of his imagination. This woman, who he has created, is in her intellectual and physical gifts a copy of man. She lives in a world that is free from silent supplications and sexual complications. If such practical thoughts ever intruded on his mind, he would of course assume that she pays her way with silent integrity, giving her full personal and financial contributions to society.

It is regarding this fictional woman that such men began to expound on the benefits that women in general would derive from full male partnership, and the benefits that such partnership would give to the community. Eventually, this inexperienced naïf sets out his idealised abstractions to persuade his reader that, by appealing purely to mental fictions, he has effectively cracked the concrete problem of gender (in)equality.

It is this, then, that is the nature of male supporters who give intellectual prestige to the feminist cause.

But in the interests of true fairness, let's ask ourselves here, is there not also a type of man who is engaged in what we like to call the business of 'the real world,' and who is not just a lukewarm opportunist but a true passionate promoter of the feminist movement? Of course there are such men – for many years I have counted some of them as close friends. But there is always for me the suspicion that such men, ardent promoters of passionate feminism in their own private lives, are idealist dreamers – ones to whom the memory of a particular woman, like Penelope for Odysseus, has taken on a mythical greatness as the emblem of an elusive happy ending.

Sorry Odysseus. Penelope got tired of waiting. She spent the last ten years bending over backwards, forwards and sideways for every last dick that swung over your threshold.

Let her go, man; and just keep on sailing.

Now we can continue to hold down, strip, and penetrate – one after another – the arguments with which female feminists try to settle the debate.

It's important to observe that the feminist never – unless she's addressing naïve little girls or dried up old crones – gets much mileage by whingeing about the legal inequalities women face. Ordinary, healthy men and women have no patience whatsoever for this kind of delusional bullshit. First, there are many who think that public benefits most, despite occasional difficulties, from existing laws; second, because any change that would be desirable could be made very easily without the use of feminism; and third, because the feminist constantly acts on the principle of depicting 'man' as absolutely evil in every regard, insisting that nothing can never be said in his favour.

The arguments that feminist women truly trust are those enshrined in general indefinite principles, formulated as axioms, disposed towards errors, vague abstract terms and questionable epithets. Normal, unsophisticated women are almost powerless to defend their minds against such arguments.

This is because they bring moral pressure to bear on human nature. If the mind is confused by a word or formula that brings an ethical appeal, it can easily engage in actions it would never have approved of through impartial reason. All such concepts as justice, social justice, freedom, chivalry – and that is what we will be especially concerned with – when misunderstood and not clearly defined, are obstacles in the way of mankind. Let us start by analysing the term "Woman's Rights" and the accompanying assertion: "Woman should have equal rights".

Our immediate focus here is on the law. We are dealing with one of the most important of verbal weapons through which the feminist hopes to put moral pressure on people.

Now the straight term in its legal sense implies a debt owed. The state owes us, its individual members, the protection needed to prevent anyone from intervening with us and preventing us from enjoying our faculties, privileges and possessions.

The term can obtain a wider meaning than this. While no-one can speak of our right to health or anything that one man does not have the power to give another, it is advisable that, independently of those prescribed by law, there are basic and inalienable rights: a right to freedom; a right to protection from personal violence; a right to the protection of our property; and a right to the impartial administration of regulations that are binding on all. Such a use of the term law can be justified on the ground that everyone is prepared to make personal sacrifices and to combine with their fellows with the purpose of ensuring these necessities.

The feminist who uses the term "women's rights" do not use the word rights in any of these senses. Her case is analogous to that of a man who has to argue in a republic about the divine right of kings; or those of the socialist who must argue that he is entitled to live permanently under a socialist government; or any member of a minority who, in order to get what he wants, argues that he is only fighting for his rights.

Under rationalist examination and scrutiny, feminist's formula of "Womens' Rights" really just equates to "Womens' Desires."

At the moment – because we are currently coming back to the issue of enforcing rights – our task is to investigate the arguments that the feminist uses to support her claims.

The first and foremost of these is the argument that "social justice" prescribes that women should be equal. When we inquire about what the feminist principle of social justice means, one only receives the answer that "social justice" is a moral principle that includes gender equality under its implications. In fact, it is only very little that clearly understands the nature of justice. For this, two very different principles are employed.

The primary and correct meaning of the term justice will probably be best addressed by pursuing the following train of considerations.

When man, longing impatiently for an objective and universal system of justice, strove to build a legal system to do the job, he built it on the following logical foundations:

(a) All crimes that the courts take note of are classified.

(b) The legal consequences of each class of crime will be determined.

(c) The courts will only argue and make decisions on the basis of facts

(d) Such decisions will automatically carry the appropriate legal consequences.

For example, if a man is arrested for murder, it is accepted that the court (when the facts are first explained) will focus only on the issue of whether the particular crime in the dispute should be classified as true murder, manslaughter, negligent homicide, or another category. This determines the sentence: the legal consequences assigned to the relevant class of action are enforced.

However, there is also another essential element in justice. It is an element that easily escapes the eye. I have the fact that the classifications accepted and embodied in the law should not be arbitrary classifications. They all need to be consistent with the principle of utility, and are aimed at the benefit of society.

For example, if an act of manslaughter is placed in the category of gross negligent homicide, it is because it is distinguished by considerations of public utility. But considerations of utility would not be present, and consequently justice would not be accepted, if we distinguished in our system of classification between murder committed by a poor man and murder committed by a rich man. Such a prejudicial concept of justice would interfere with the considerations of utility and equity.

It is clear that if we regard the justice administered in the courts, we can call it rightful justice. Then the only remaining question is whether it is in the public interest to legally grant full equality to women, classifying them as the equal of and equivalent to men in every respect.

There is another principle under the name of 'social justice' as already indicated. I have in mind the conviction that in the distribution of wealth or political power, or any other privileges that exist in society, everyone should share equally with every other man and every woman. In countries where Europeans and non-Europeans live next to each other, this latter must share all privileges equally with the first. The aim of the principle is to eliminate all distinctions that are dependent on natural endowment, gender and race.

This principle aims to establish proper artificial equality; it appeals to our ethical instincts and claims that the distinctions of formal law are taken into account.

But to take the principle to its logical conclusion, it would of course have to embrace all life on earth – not just humans, but also the lower animals. That is to say, if the principal of 'social justice' were followed to its logical extent, then we would all of us be forced to become feminists; then human rights lawyers; then, by means of a logical compulsion, animal rights activists; then vegans; and finally obsessive radicals like the unhinged Jain cult in India, who avoid even breathing in fruitflies out of their misguided idealism.

If we accept this principle of equality of justice as an absolute obligation, we must believe and encourage all the other insane and dangerous "isms" represented in the ranks of women feminists.

If, on the other hand, we accept the doctrine of social justice with the qualification that it will only apply as far as it is in accordance with the public good, we will again make practicality the criterion of the justice of feminism.

Before moving on, it would be best to emphasise that the spectre of social justice comes to us not only in the form that justice requires women have full equality, but also in other forms. We meet it in the writings of humanitarian publicists, we meet it in the streets, on the crudely scrawled banners of feminist protesters.

It is ironic that the very income that female feminists squander on the slander of man are to a large extent derived from funds he has earned and given to the woman. As regards the financial situation of women as set out here, the claim of equality for the rich woman should first be considered.

We can look for illumination on the logical and moral aspects of this claim by considering a case study. The position occupied in society by the woman who inherited her money is similar to that occupied in a company by a sleeping partner who has little capital in the company business. If such a partner claimed financial control and had to make an effort to pay its royalties on a pro rata basis, he would be very strongly called to order. And he would never think of appealing to justice by protesting in the streets, breaking windows, biting the hand that feeds.

Just as for socialism, it is really about trying to control the money of others. And in the case of women, it is asserting in relation to her public partnership with man this inventive principle of domestic partnership: "What's yours is mine, and what's mine is also mine". The feminist marriage vow, if you will!

Alongside her insistence on 'social justice', the most pressing advocacy on the part of the woman is her insistence on "freedom".

Here again we have a word that is a valuable asset for feminism, both in respect to moral pressure and respect as a word of ambiguous meaning. Everywhere in the literature of feminism, we speak of the "emancipation" of woman; and we have women characterised as servants, or slaves.

When we have managed to penetrate through this thick hymen of lies, we find that the idea of freedom floating before the eyes of women is not a question of freedom in relation to unfair legal constraints, but rather a sort of freedom which focuses on the possession of money which confers liberation from sexual constraints.

The feminist agitator takes advantage of this ambiguity. By addressing the worker who, at the rate that her job commands on the market, does not earn enough to give her a reasonable financial freedom, the agitator will assure her that feminism will bring her more money, describing feminism as the cause of liberty, cunningly juggling with two different senses of the word "freedom".

Equality, however, would not increase the wages of the worker and would bring her neither the financial nor the sexual freedom she seeks.

The tactic of feminist agitators is the same when dealing with a woman who lives at the expense of a husband or a parent and who shrinks from the idea that she is under a moral obligation to return to the man who works for her a reward of gratitude. The feminist agitator will tell her that such an obligation is slavery and that the cause of feminism is the cause of freedom.

I am, as I write these very words, more than two years into a prison sentence. Every day I suffer a thousand small indignities at the hands of my fellow prisoners, guards, visitors, and anyone who sees fit to take advantage of my current situation. Yet I honestly believe that, if my ex-wife ever took the time to visit me in this godforsaken place, she would find some subtle way to let me know that somehow I still don't have it as bad as she did when we lived together. Somehow, even now, I still don't have the right to feel aggrieved. Somehow, even though she had every material want provided for, a beautiful son, a loving (if imperfect) husband – despite all that, as a married woman, she was far more downtrodden and abused than I am right now.

And so we find that women who want everything for nothing, and women who do not believe they are indebted to men for anything, and who consider that they have not made a sufficiently good life for themselves – in short, all ungrateful women – flock to the banner of women's freedom – the banner of financial freedom for women at the expense of slavery for man.

The truly grateful woman will almost always be an anti-feminist.

It would be good, before moving on to another class of arguments, to summarise what was said in the previous three sections.

We have recognised that women have not been cheated of basic natural rights; that true justice, distinct from "social justice," does not prescribe that she be admitted to full equality; and that woman's status is not, as is dishonestly claimed, a status of servitude or slavery.

With that, the whole affair of recrimination against man, let alone the case for resorting to protest, collapses. And if it breaks down, it's one of those things that has consequences. It should be remembered that giving in to an unjustified and dubious claim is to serve the demoralization of the plaintiff.

3. Do women have any genuine grievances?

We move from the argument of elementary natural rights to another class of arguments – intellectual grievances. The feminist tells us that it is incongruous to oppose feminism; that it is insulting to tell the woman that she is incapable of complete equality; that it is "illogical" to make in its case an exception to a general rule; that it is a mere "prejudice" to deny her equality; and, finally, that it is an affront that a woman should be required to obey "artificial" laws.

Let's take these in order.

Consider chivalry, first, from the feminist's point of view. Her notion of chivalry is that man should accept any disadvantageous offer that can be made by a woman.

Of course, this definition of chivalry is a total distortion of the principle of "equality", fiercely biased in its application to the cases of men and women.

But to do feminist justice, she does not support the argument of chivalry. Insofar as life has made her understand that the ordinary man has other conceptions of this virtue, she declares that she "does not need it."

Let us now turn to the anti-feminist point of view. The anti-feminist (male or female) believes that chivalry is a principle that involves every serious relationship between the sexes and all the civilizing organizations in the world that are most important.

But I think I hear the reader interpose, "What, then, is chivalry if it is not a question of serving woman without reward?"

A moment's thought will make the matter clear.

When a man makes this compact with a woman, "I will do you reverence, and protect you, and yield you service; and you, for your part, will hold fast to an ideal of gentleness, of personal refinement, of modesty, of joyous maternity, and to who shall say what other graces and virtues that endear woman to man," that is *chivalry*.

It is not a question of a purely one-sided bargain, as in the feminist conception. Nor yet is it a bargain about purely material things. It is a bargain in which man gives both material things, and also things which pertain perhaps somewhat to the spirit; and in which woman gives back of the latter.

But nonetheless it is of the nature of a contract. The contract is infringed when woman breaks out into violence, when she jettisons her personal refinement, when she is ungrateful, and, possibly, when she places a quite extravagantly high estimate upon her intellectual powers.

Suppose that a husband loves his wife, of several years. Suppose he dotes on her, is only very rarely unfaithful, gives her everything she needs to be happy – because she is the image of perfection in his eyes. Is it the man's fault if he loses interest in this woman, after she apparently loses interest in herself? If she stops exercising, adopts an unhealthy diet, sinks into a general lethargy, talks behind his back... Can we blame this man for straying? Can we blame him for feeling that he – and not his wife – has been in some way 'cheated'?

We must now turn from these almost too intimate questions of personal morality to discuss the other grievances enumerated above. With regard to the feminist's complaint that it is *"insulting"* for woman to be told that she is as a class unfit to enjoy full equality, it is relevant to point out that to be "insulted" is to be told about oneself, or one's class, untruths – not truths which one dislikes.

And it is, of course, an offence against ethics to try to dispose of an unpalatable generalisation by characterising it as "insulting." But nothing that man could do would be likely to prevent the feminist resorting to this aggravated form of intellectual immorality.

We may now turn to the complaint that it is "illogical" to withhold equality from women. This is the kind of complaint which truly brings out the logical endowment and legislative wisdom of the feminist. With regard to her logical endowment it will suffice to indicate that the feminist would appear to regard the essence of logic as "rules have no exception".

Can an "offensive," but rationally valid, generalisation legitimately be dismissed by characterising it as a *prejudice*? This is a fundamentally important question not only in connection with such an issue as feminism, but in connection with all searches for truth in those regions where crucial scientific experiments cannot be instituted. In the whole of this region of thought we have to guide ourselves by generalisations.

Now every generalisation is in a sense a *prejudgment*. We make inferences from cases or individuals that have already presented themselves to such cases or individuals of the same class as may afterwards present themselves. And if our generalisation happens to be an unfavourable one, we shall of necessity have prejudged the case against those who are exceptions to their class.

Thus, for example, the proposition that women are incapable of usefully serving on the front lines of a military prejudges the case against a certain number of capable women. It would none the less be absolutely anarchical to propose to abandon the system of guiding ourselves by prejudgments; and unfavourable prejudgments or prejudices are logically as well justified, and are obviously as indispensable to us as favourable prejudgments.

There is, therefore, only one reasonable response to the feminist who proposes to dispose of generalisations which are unfavourable to woman as prejudices.

"Shut up".

It has probably never suggested itself to her that, if there were a mind which was not stored with both favourable prejudgments and prejudices, it would be a mind which had learned absolutely nothing from experience.

But I hear the reader interpose, "Is there not a grave danger that generalisations may be erroneous?" And I can also hear that high-pitched, nagging voice again; "Is there not a grave danger that unflattering generalisations about women may be erroneous?"

The answer to the general question is that there is of course always the risk that our generalisations may be erroneous. But when a generalisation finds wide acceptance among a large body of thoughtful and educated men, we have come as close to truth as it is possible for humanity to come.

To the question put by this familiar high-pitched, whining voice, the reply must be that lived experience with regard to the capacity of woman has been accumulating throughout the history of mankind; and that, throughout all that time, the belief of most men in the inherent inferiority of women in terms of intellectual and moral development has never wavered.

We have come now to the last item on our list, to the grievance that woman has to submit herself to *"manmade laws."* This is a grievance which well rewards study. It is worth study from the feminist point of view, because it is the one great injury under which all others are subsumed. And it is worth studying from the Egalitarian point of view, because it shows how little the feminist understands of the terms she employs; and how unreal are the wrongs which she resents.

This feminist tendency to misunderstand this particular point is quite incredible. The feminist misapprehends – it will be better to assume that she "misapprehends" – when she suggests that we, the male arbiters of society, have framed the laws.

In reality the law which we live under – and the law in those societies which have adopted or imitated Western democracy – descends from the past. It has been evolved precedent upon precedent, by the decisions of generation upon generation of judges, and it has for centuries been purged by amending statutes. Moreover we, the present male electors – the electors who are savagely attacked by the feminist for our asserted iniquities in connection with the laws which regulate sexual relations – have never in our capacity as electors had any power to alter an old, or to suggest a new law; except by voting for this party or the other, through which we may indirectly have remotely influenced the general trend of legislation.

"Well, but" – the feminist will here shrilly reply – "is it not true that in the drafting of statutes and the framing of judicial decisions man has always unfairly discriminated against woman?"

The question really supplies its own answer. It will be obvious to everyone who considers that the drafting of statutes and the formulating of legal decisions is almost as impersonal a procedure as that of drawing up the rules to govern a game; and it offers hardly more opportunity for discriminating between man and woman. There are, however, two issues in connection with which the law can and does make a distinction between man and woman.

The *first* is that of rape. Not only are the legal penalties for rape sufficiently harsh; in many European countries, including the one from which I write, penalties are imposed which far outstrip anything that could reasonably called 'proportionate' – and the definition of "rape" itself has been stretched to the point of total meaninglessness. There are strong, proud men languishing in prisons all over this land, who not only present no threat to good and proper Swedish women, but constitute their only hope for salvation from the dark, animalistic tide even now rushing over this country's borders.

It is also worth shining a light on the still-widespread falsehood that 'rape' is something which only happens to women. It is a matter of clinical record that men are raped – not just by other men, but by women also – in a wide variety of settings. By the same token as that with which she argues against the validity of generalisation, the feminist will attempt to dismiss this fact as irrelevant; citing the received wisdom that there are "far fewer" rapes of men than there are rapes of women, and that the vast majority are committed by other men in the setting of penal institutions.

If this doesn't illustrate the unflinching, self-serving ruthlessness of the modern feminist, nothing will. What kind of person could look into the tearful (while still manly and resolute) eyes of a male rape victim and tell him – with all sincerity, and in that now all-too-familiar, shrill and womanly voice – "Your suffering does not count"?

The *second* point in which the law differentiates is in the matter of exacting personal service for society. If it had not been that man is more prone to discriminate in favour of woman than against her, every military, when exacting personal service from men, would have demanded the equivalent from women. As it is, the militaries of various Western countries currently go through the motions of sham equality – letting women tell themselves they are doing the work of men, while still coddling and sequestering them for their own much-needed protection.

The feminist further misapprehends when she regards it as an indignity to obey laws which she has not herself framed, or specifically sanctioned. (The whole male electorate, be it remarked, would here lie under the same dignity as woman.)

But in reality, whether it is a question of the rules of a game, or of the reciprocal rights and duties of members of a community, it is, and ought to be, to every reasonable human being not a grievance, but a reason for celebration, that an expert or a body of experts should have evolved a set of rules under which order and harmony are achieved. Only vanity and folly would counsel amateurs to try to draw up rules or laws for themselves.

Again, the woman feminist takes it as a matter of course that she would herself be able to construct a system of workable laws. In point of fact, the framing of a really useful law is a question of divining something which will apply to an infinite number of different cases and individuals. It is an intellectual feat on a par with the framing of a great generalisation. And would woman – being of such short sight, whose mind is always so taken up with whatever instances lie nearest to her – be capable of framing anything that could pass muster as a great generalisation?

Lastly, the feminist fails to see that the function of framing the laws is not an essential function of citizenship. The essential functions of citizenship are the shaping of public policy, and the control of the administrative Acts of Government. Such directive control is in a state of political freedom exercised through two quite different agencies.

It is exercised – and it is of the very essence of political freedom that this should be the normal method of control – in the first place, through expressed public opinion. By this are continuously regulated not only momentous matters of State, such as declarations of war and the introduction of constitutional changes, but also smaller and more individual matters, such as the commutation of a capital sentence, or the appropriate use of police force when suppressing militant feminist protests.

With this I have, I will not say completed the tale of the feminist's grievances – that would be impossible – but I have at any rate dealt with those which she has most acrimoniously insisted upon.

4. 'Fake it till we make it'?

There remains still a further class of arguments. I have in view here arguments which have nothing to do with elementary rights, nor yet with hurt feelings. They concern ethics, sympathy, and self-improvement.

The feminists here argue that woman, being more disadvantaged by society, needs equality for her protection; and secondly that women must be given central roles in all areas of society first, in order to advance as a gender.

Suppose that a woman is ill. Should we go to her and say: "You know best, better than any man, what is wrong with you. Here are all the medicines – here's a whole hospital, and all its staff, at your personal disposal. We'll even paint it a pretty shade of pink! Choose your own course of treatment, lady, for that will definitely be the one most likely to help."

Seems pretty futile, if not inhumane, doesn't it? Gender is no guarantee of insight or wisdom. What would really help the sick woman would, of course, be to have the best and brightest doctor in the hospital decide for himself how she should be treated, and submit to his will absolutely.

If a man has a wife whom he desires to indulge, he doesn't necessarily open a joint bank account with her. If he wants to contribute to a charity he does not give to the managers of that charity a power of attorney over his property.

If he is a wealthy philanthropist, the CEO of a great corporation, when one pathetically poor employee among his staff is brought to his notice, he doesn't imperil the fortunes of his company by giving all his workmen shares in the management. Moreover, he would perhaps regard it as a little suspect if a group of those who were claiming this as a right came and told him that "it was very selfish of him" not to grant their request.

Invaluable to the radical feminist, and every other woman who wants to get at the balls of a man, is that word "selfish". It furnishes her with the *petitio principii* that man is under an ethical obligation to give anything she chooses to ask.

Making a woman a doctor will not automatically make her a healer. Making a woman prime minister does not make her a leader. Making a woman your wife does not make her faithful. Sorry, kiddies – wishing for something does not make it real. In this world, that is accomplished through blood, sweat, struggle, and balls.

PART II – The Truth

1. Inconvenient fact: some women are weak

The feminist movement has now gone too far to be disposed of by such a small thing as a complete, rational dismantling of its arguments. The situation demands that the case against feminism be made as forcefully as possible; and it must be the full and quite unexpurgated case.

I shall endeavour to do this in the fewest possible words, and to be more especially brief where I have to pass again over ground which I have previously traversed in dealing with the arguments of the feminists. Let us begin with the fundamentals.

It is an axiom that we should in legislating guide ourselves directly by considerations of utility and expediency. For abstract principles – I have in view here rights, justice, egalitarian equity, equality, liberty, chivalry, logicality, and such like – are not all of them guides to utility; and each of these is, as we have seen, open to all manner of private misinterpretation.

Applying the above axiom to the issue before us, it is clear that we ought to confine ourselves here to the discussion of the question as to whether society would, or would not, suffer from the admission of women to full equality.

We can arrive at a judgment upon this by considering, on the one hand, the class-characters of women so far as these may be relevant to the question of feminist activism; and, on the other hand, the legislative programmes put forward by the female SJW and the feminist.

In connection with the class-characters of woman, it will be well, before attempting to indicate them, to interpolate here the general consideration that the practical statesman, who has to deal with things as they are, is not required to decide whether the characters of women which will here be considered are, as the physiologist (who knows that the sexual products influence every tissue of the body) cannot doubt, "secondary sexual characters"; or, as the feminist contends, "acquired characters." It will be plain that whether defects are "secondary sexual characters" (and therefore as irremediable as "racial characters"); or whether they are "acquired characters" (and as such theoretically remediable) they are relevant to the question of the concession of feminist activism just so long as they continue to be exhibited.

The primordial argument against struggling to give woman full equality is that, on a physiological level, it is not possible to give it to them in the only area which truly matters – that of physical force.

Now it is by physical force alone and by prestige – which represents physical force in the background – that a nation protects itself against foreign interference, upholds its rule over subject populations, and enforces its own laws. And nothing could in the end more certainly lead to war and revolt than the decline of the military spirit and loss of prestige which would inevitably follow if man admitted woman into complete social and political co-partnership.

While it is arguable that such a partnership with woman in government as has already been allowed in Western nations is sufficiently unreal to be endurable, there cannot be two opinions on the question that a virile and imperial race will not brook any attempt at forcible control by women.

Again, no military foreign nation or native people will ever believe in the stamina and firmness of purpose of any nation that submitted even to the semblance of such control. It is to the rise of female political involvement in the west that many leading thinkers attribute the increased hostility of nations such as Russia and North Korea. Simply put, such nations rightly have no respect or fear for a nation of men who have let their women cut off their balls in the name of 'equality'.

The general lesson that all governmental action ought to be backed by force, is further brought home to the conscience when we take note of the fact that everyone feels that public morality is affronted when senile, infirm, and bedridden men are given political power, instead of their younger, more virile counterparts.

For electoral decisions are felt to have moral prestige only when the electoral figures quantitatively represent the physical forces which are engaged on either side. And where vital interests are involved, no class of men can be expected to accept any decision other than one which rests upon the *ultima ratio.*

Now all the evils which are the outcome of disparities between the parliamentary power and the organised physical force of contending parties would "grow" a hundredfold if women were allowed to put into full practice the principle of feminist activism.

There would after that be no electoral or parliamentary decision which would not be open to challenge on the ground that it was impossible to tell whether the party which came out the winner had a majority which could enforce its will, or only a majority obtained by the inclusion of women. And no measure of redistribution could ever set that right.

Coming back in conclusion to our main issue, I would re-emphasise an aspect of the question upon which I have already elsewhere insisted. I have in view the fact that woman does, and should, stand to physical violence in a fundamentally different relation to man. Nothing can alter the fact that, the very moment woman resorts to violence, she places herself within the jurisdiction of an ethical law as old as civilisation, and which was framed in its interests.

"If you throw a punch at me, little girl, I will block it," says Society. "If you throw another, little girl, I will throw one back. Block it if you can."

2. Inconvenient fact: some women are stupid

The woman with full equality would be an absurd danger to society not only because she could not back her opinions by physical force, but also by reason of her intellectual defects. Woman's mind attends in appraising a statement primarily to the mental images which it evokes, and only secondarily – and sometimes not at all – to what is predicated in the overall good of society.

It is over-influenced by individual instances; arrives at conclusions on incomplete evidence; has a very imperfect sense of proportion; accepts the congenial as true, and rejects the uncongenial as false; takes the imaginary which is desired for reality, and treats the undesired reality which is out of sight as non-existent – building up for itself in this way, when biased by predilections and aversions, a very unreal picture of the external world.

The explanation of this is to be found in all the physiological attachments of woman's mind: in the fact that mental images are in her over-intimately linked up with emotional reflex responses; that yielding to such reflex responses gives gratification; that intellectual analysis and suspense of judgment involve an inhibition of reflex responses which is felt as neural distress; that precipitate judgment brings relief from this physiological strain; and that woman looks upon her mind not as an implement for the pursuit of truth, but as an instrument for providing her with creature comforts in the form of agreeable mental images.

In order to satisfy the physical yearning for such comforts, a considerable section of intelligent and virtuous women insist on picturing to themselves that the reign of physical force is over, or as good as over; that distinctions based upon physical and intellectual force may be reckoned as non-existent; that male supremacy as resting upon these is a thing of the past; and that

Justice means Egalitarian Equity – means equating the weaklings with the strong and the incapable with the capable.

All this because these particular ideas are congenial to the woman of refinement, and because it is to her, when she is a feminist, uncongenial that there should exist another principle of justice which demands from the physically and intellectually capable that they shall retain the reins of government in their own hands; and specially uncongenial that in all man-governed States the ideas of justice of the more forceful should have worked out so much to the advantage of women, that a large majority of these are indifferent or actively hostile to the feminism movement.

In further illustration of what has been said above, it may be pointed out that woman, even intelligent woman, nurses all sorts of misconceptions about herself. She, for instance, is constantly picturing to herself that she can as a worker lay claim to the same all-round efficiency as a man – forgetting that woman is notoriously unadapted to tasks in which severe physical hardships have to be confronted; and that hardly anyone would, if other alternative offered, employ a woman in any work which imposed upon her a combined physical and mental strain, or in any work where emergencies might have to be faced.

In like manner the feminist is fond of picturing to herself that woman is for all ordinary purposes the intellectual equal, and that the intelligent woman is the superior of the ordinary man.

These results are arrived at by fixing the attention upon the fact that an ordinary man and an ordinary woman are, from the point of view of memory and apprehension, very much on a level; and that a highly intelligent woman has a quicker memory and a more rapid power of apprehension than the ordinary men; and further, by leaving out of regard that it is not so much a quick memory or a rapid power of apprehension which is required for effective intellectual work, as originality, or at any rate independence of thought, a faculty of felicitious generalisations and diacritical judgment, long-sustained intellectual effort, an unselective mirroring of the world in the mind, and that relative immunity to fallacy which goes together with a stable and comparatively unresponsive nervous system.

When we consider that the intellect of the quite ungifted man works with this last-mentioned physiological advantage, we can see that the male intellect must be, and – pace the woman feminist – it in point of fact is, within its range, a better instrument for dealing with the practical affairs of life than that of the intelligent woman.

How far off we are in the case of woman from an unselective mirroring of the world in the mind is shown by the fact that large and important factors of life may be represented in woman's mind by lacunae of which she is totally unconscious.

Thus, for instance, that not very unusual type of spinster who is in a condition of retarded development (and you will find this kind of woman even on County Councils), is completely unconscious of the sexual element in herself and in human nature generally. Try as you might, you cannot bring it home to her that unsatisfied sexuality is an intellectual disability.

Sufficient illustration will now have been given of woman's incapacity to take a complete or objective view of any matter in which she has a personal, or any kind of emotional interest; and this would now be the place to discuss those other aspects of her mind which are relevant to her claim to feminist activism. I refer to her logical endowment and her political sagacity.

All that I might have been required to say here on these issues has, however, already been said by me in dealing with the arguments of the feminist. I have there carefully written it in between the lines.

One thing only remains over. We must, before we pass on, consider whether woman has really, as she tells us, given earnest for the future weeding out of these her secondary sexual characters, by making quite phenomenal advances within the lifetime of the present generation; and, above all, whether there is any basis for woman's confident assurance that, when for a few generations she shall have enjoyed educational advantages, she will at any rate pull up level with man. The vision of the future may first engage our attention; for only this roseate prospect makes of any man a feminist.

We have to consider here whether "survival of the fittest" really furnishes scientific basis for the belief that educational advantages carried on from generation to generation will level up woman's intellect to man's; and whether, as the feminist also believes, the narrow education of past generations of women can be held responsible for their present intellectual shortcomings.

A moment's consideration will show – for we may here fix our eyes only on the future – that woman could not hope to advance relatively to man except upon the condition that the acquired characteristics of woman, instead of being handed down equally to her male and female descendants, were accumulated upon her daughters.

Now if that be a law of heredity, it is a law which is as yet unheard of outside the sphere of the feminist societies. Moreover, one is accustomed to hear women, when they are not arguing on feminist activism, allege that clever mothers make clever sons.

It must, as it will have come home to us, be clear to every thoughtful mind that woman's belief that she will, through education and the accumulation of its effects upon her through generations, become a more glorious being, rests, not upon any rational basis, but only on the physiological fact that what is congenial to woman impresses itself upon her as true.

All that sober science in the form of history and physiology would seem to entitle us to hope from the future of woman is that she will develop *pari passu* with man; and that education will teach her not to retard him overmuch by her lagging in the rear.

In view of this larger issue, the question as to whether woman has, in any real sense of the word, been making progress in the course of the present generation, loses much of interest.

If to move about more freely, to read more freely, to speak out her mind more freely, and to have emancipated herself from traditionary beliefs – and, I would add, traditionary ethics – is to have advanced, woman has indubitably advanced. But educated men in the Middle East too have advanced in all these respects; and they also tell us that they are pulling up level with citizens of Western democracy.

Let us at any rate, when the feminist is congratulating herself on her own progress, meditate also upon that dictum of Nietzsche, "Progress is writ large on all woman's banners and bannerets; but one can actually see her going back."

3. Inconvenient fact: some women are liars

Yet a third point has to come into consideration in connection with the hypothetical 'equal' woman. This is, that she would be pernicious to society also by virtue of her defective moral equipment.

Let me make clear what is the nature of the defect of morality which is here imputed to woman. Conduct may be appraised by very different standards. We may appraise it by reference to a transcendental religious ideal which demands that the physical shall be subordinated to the spiritual, and that the fetters of self should be flung aside.

Or again, we may bring into application purely mundane utilitarian standards, and may account conduct as immoral or moral according as it seeks only the happiness of the agent, or the happiness of the narrow circle of humanity which includes along with him also his relatives and intimate friends, or again, the welfare of the wider circle which includes all those with whom he may have come into contact, or whom he may affect through his work; or again, the welfare of the whole body-politic of which we are members; or lastly, that of the general body of mankind.

Now it might be contended that all these different moralities are in their essence one and the same; and that one cannot comply with the requirements of any one of these systems of morality without fulfilling in a measure the requirements of all the other moralities.

It might, for example, be urged that if a man strive after the achievement of a transcendental ideal in which self shall be annulled, he will *pro tanto* be bringing welfare to his domestic circle; or again, that it would be impossible to promote domestic welfare without, through this, promoting the welfare of the nation, and through that the general welfare of the world.

In like manner it might be argued that all work done for abstract principles of morality like liberty and justice, for the advancement of knowledge, and for whatever else goes to the building up of a higher civilisation, will, by promoting the welfare of the general body of mankind, redound to the advantage of each several nation, and ultimately to the advantage of each domestic circle.

But all this would be true only in a very superficial and strictly qualified sense. In reality, just as there is eternal conflict between egoism and altruism, so there is conflict between the different moralities.

To take examples, the attempt to actualise the transcendental religious ideal may, when pursued with ardour, very easily conflict with the morality which makes domestic felicity its end. And again – as we see in the pacifist movement, in the history of the early Christian Church, in the case of the Quakers and in the teachings of Tolstoy – it may quite well set itself in conflict with national ideals, and dictate a line of conduct which is, from the point of view of society, immoral.

We need no further witness of the divorce between idealistic and national morality than that which is supplied in the memorable truism, "No state which was conducted on truly democratic principles could hold together for a day." And domestic morality will constantly come into conflict with public morality.

To do everything in one's power to advance one's relatives and friends irrespectively of all considerations of merit would, no doubt, be quite sound domestic morality; it could, however, not always be reconciled with public morality. In the same way, to take one's country's part in all eventualities would be patriotic, but it might quite well conflict with the higher interests of humanity.

Now, the point towards which we have been winning our way is that each man's moral station and degree will be determined by the election which he makes where egoism and altruism, and where a narrower and a wider code of morality, conflict.

That the moral law forbids yielding to the promptings of egoism or to those of the narrower moralities when this involves a violation of the precepts of the wider morality is axiomatic. Criminal and anti-social actions are not excused by the fact that motives which impelled their commission were not purely egoistic.

But the ethical law demands more than abstention from definitely anti-social actions. It demands from every individual that he shall recognise the precepts of public morality as of superior obligation to those of egoism and domestic morality.

By the fact that her public men recognised this ethical law Rome won for herself in the ancient world spectacular grandeur. By an unexampled national obedience to it glory has in our time accrued to Japan. And, in truth, there is not anywhere any honour or renown but such as comes from casting away the bonds of self and of the narrower moralities to carry out the behests of the wider morality.

Even in the strongholds of transcendental religion where it was axiomatic that morality began and was summed up in personal morality, it is gradually coming to be recognised that, where we have two competing moralities, it is always the wider morality which has the prior claim upon our allegiance.

A common protest against the morality of "saving one's dirty soul" marks a step forwards. And we find full recognition of the superior claim of the larger morality in the following virile dictum, "I would rather have Britain free, than Britain sober." This I am proud to say I coined myself, during a particularly venomous exchange with my ex-wife while our son (my son) was sleeping soundly in the next room. Having returned from a wholesome night of heterosexual carousing with a few long-term male friends, I found her waiting up for me. She could not believe, would not accept, that the evening had been representative of a normal, healthy, and entirely natural male form of pressure relief.

In her mind, the "law" of her own hurt feelings by far outweighed the 'law' of nature by which four heterosexual men, drunk on the intoxication of liquor and each others' company, might take a few brief hours out of the working week to give each other succor. To soothe the pangs of working men, forced to endure not only the rigours of manual and intellectual labour, but the burden of their wives' constant judgment and scrutiny.

I did not lay hands on her that night, or any other night while we were married – despite her many insinuations to the contrary, which succeeded in their goal of doing real damage to my personal reputation and professional prospects. I hope she knows how grateful she ought to be for my restraint.

What is here new, let it be noted, is only the acknowledgment by those whose official allegiance is to a transcendental ideal of personal morality that they are called upon to obey a higher allegiance. For there has always existed, in the doctrine that guilty man could not be pardoned and taken back into favour until the claims of eternal justice had been satisfied, theoretical recognition of the principle that one must conform to the precepts of abstract morality before one may ethically indulge oneself in the lower moralities of philanthropy and personal benevolence.

The viewpoint from which I would propose to survey the morality of woman has now been reached. It has, however, still to be pointed out that we may appropriately, in comparing the morals of man and woman, confine our survey to a comparatively narrow field. That is to say, we may here rule out all that relates to purely personal and domestic morality – for this is not relevant to feminist activism. And we may also rule out all that relates to offences against the police laws – such as public drunkenness and offences against the criminal law – for these would come into consideration only in connection with an absolutely inappreciable fraction of voters.

It will be well to begin by highlighting certain points in the moral psychology of man.

When morality takes up its abode in a man who belongs to the intellectual caste it will show itself in his becoming mindful of his public obligations. He will consider the quality of his work as affecting the interest of those who have to place dependence upon it; behaviour to those who are casually brought into relations with him; the discharge of his indebtedness to the community; and the proper conduct of public affairs.

In particular, it will be to him a matter of concern that the law shall be established upon classifications which are just (in the sense of being conformable to public advantage); and that the laws shall everywhere be justly, that is to say rigorously and impartially, administered.

If we now turn to the man in the street we shall not find him especially sensible to the appeals of morality. But when the special call comes it will generally be possible to trust him: as an elector, to vote uninfluenced by considerations of private advantage; and, when called to serve on a jury, to apply legal classifications without distinction of person.

Furthermore, in all times of crisis he may be counted upon to apply the principles of communal morality which have been handed down in the race.

Lastly, we come to the man who is intolerant of all the ordinary restraints of personal and domestic morality. Even in him the seeds of communal morality will often be found deeply implanted.

Time and again a regiment of scumbags, who have let all other morality go hang, have, when the proper chord has been made to vibrate in them, heard the call of communal morality, and done deeds which make the ears of whoever hears of them tingle.

We come into an entirely different land when we come to the morality of woman. It is personal and domestic, not public, morality which is instinctive in her.

In other words, when egoism gives ground to altruism, that altruism is exercised towards those who are linked up to her by a bond of sexual affection, or a community in blood, or failing this, by a relation of personal friendship, or by some other personal relation. And even when altruism has had her perfect work, woman feels no interest in, and no responsibility towards, any abstract moral ideal.

And though the feminist may protest, instancing in disproof of this her own burning enthusiasm for justice, we, for our part, may legitimately ask whether evidence of a moral enthusiasm for justice would be furnished by a desire to render to others their due, or by vehement insistence upon one's own rights, and systematic attempts to extort, under the cover of the word "justice," advantages for oneself.

But it will be well to dwell a little longer on, and to bring out more clearly, the point that woman's moral ideals are personal and domestic, as distinguished from impersonal and public.

Let us note in this connection that it would be difficult to conceive of a woman who had become deaf to the appeal of personal and domestic morality making it a matter of honour to respond to a call of public morality; and difficult to conceive of a woman recovering lost self-respect by fulfilling such an obligation. But one knows that woman will rise and respond to the call of any strong human or transcendental personal affection.

Again, it is only a very exceptional woman who would, when put to her election between the claims of a narrow and domestic and a wider or public morality, subordinate the former to the latter.

In ordinary life, at any rate, one finds her following in such a case the suggestions of domestic – I had almost called it animal – morality.

It would be difficult to find any one who would trust a woman to be just to the rights of others in the case where the material interests of her children, or of a devoted husband, were involved. And even to consider the question of being in such a case intellectually just to any one who came into competition with personal belongings like husband and child would, of course, lie quite beyond the moral horizon of ordinary woman.

There is between man and woman here a characteristic difference. In societal terms, one would not be very far from the truth if one alleged that there are no good women, but only women who have lived under the influence of good men.

Even more serious than this postponement of public to private morality is the fact that even reputedly ethical women will, in the interests of what they take to be idealistic causes, violate laws which are universally accepted as being of moral obligation.

I here pass over the recent epidemic of political crime among women to advert to the want of conscience which permits, in connection with professedly idealistic causes, not only misrepresentations, but the making of deliberately false statements on matters of public concern.

It is, for example, an illustration of the profoundly different moral atmospheres in which men and women live that when a woman journalist recently made, for what was to her an idealistic purpose, a deliberately false statement of fact in *The Times*, she quite naively confessed to it, seeing nothing whatever amiss in her action.

And it did not appear that any other woman feminist could discern any kind of immorality in it. The worst thing they could find to say was that it perhaps was a little gauche to confess to making a deliberately false statement on a public question when it was for the moment particularly desirable that woman should show up to best advantage before the eyes of man.

We may now for a moment put aside the question of woman's public morality and consider a question which is inextricably mixed up with the question of the admission of woman to full equality. This is the mental attitude and the programme of the female SJW.

4. Inconvenient fact: feminism is a mental illness

For man the physiological psychology of woman is full of difficulties. He is not a little mystified when he encounters in her periodically recurring phases of hypersensitiveness, unreasonableness, and loss of the sense of proportion.

He is frankly perplexed when confronted with a complete alteration of character in a woman who is with child.

When he is a witness of the "tendency of woman to morally warp when nervously ill," and of the terrible physical havoc which the pangs of a disappointed love may work, he is appalled.

And it leaves on his mind an eerie feeling when he sees serious and long-continued mental disorders developing in connection with the approaching extinction of a woman's reproductive faculty.

No man can close his eyes to these things; but he does not feel at liberty to speak of them. For the woman that God gave him is not his to give away. As for woman herself, she makes very light of any of these mental upsets. She perhaps smiles a little at them...

Nonetheless, these upsets of her mental equilibrium are the things that a woman has most cause to fear; and no doctor can ever lose sight of the fact that the mind of woman is always threatened with danger from the reverberations of her physiological emergencies.

It is with such thoughts that the doctor lets his eyes rest upon the militant feminist. He cannot shut them to the fact that there is mixed up with the woman's movement much mental disorder; and he cannot conceal from himself the physiological emergencies which lie behind.

The recruiting field for militant feminists is the millions of our excess female population – those millions which should long ago have gone out to mate with its complement of men beyond the sea.

Among them there are the following different types of women:

(a) First – let us put them first – come a class of women who hold, with minds otherwise unwarped, that they may, whenever it is to their advantage, lawfully resort to physical violence. The programme, as distinguished from the methods, of these women is not very different from that of the ordinary feminist woman.

(b) There file past next a class of women who have all their lives been strangers to joy, women in whom instincts long suppressed have in the end broken into flame. These are the sexually embittered women in whom everything has turned into gall and bitterness of heart, and hatred of men. Their legislative programme is license for themselves, or else restrictions for man.

(c) Next there file past the incomplete. One side of their nature has undergone atrophy, with the result that they have lost touch with their living fellow men and women. Their programme is to convert the whole world into a neutered institution – a neutered institution in which man and woman shall everywhere work side by side at the selfsame tasks and for the selfsame pay.

These wishes can never by any possibility be realised. Even in animals – I say even, because in these at least one of the sexes has periods of complete quiescence – male and female cannot be safely worked side by side, except when they are incomplete.

While in the human species safety can be obtained, it can be obtained only at the price of continual constraint. And even then woman, though she protests that she does not require it, and that she does not receive it, practically always does receive differential treatment at the hands of man.

It is hard to describe to single men just how unnatural it is for a red-blooded, heterosexual man – with those awful, unclean, criminal balls dangling down between his thighs – to suppress the urge to bed and pursue women besides his lady wife. If my ex-wife only knew how many bold and raging erections I had suppressed while lusting after passing girls, in her name, and for her sake, her gratitude would rightly be overwhelming.

Perhaps, if she knew how numerous and strong and hard those neglected surges of passion were, she would be a little more understanding about their absence at other times. Perhaps she would reflect a little more on her own culpability for those absences, and the dwindling of passion they represented. Perhaps she would have that wisdom. But, based on painful lived experience and hard-won wisdom, I severely doubt it.

It would be well, I often think, that every woman should be clearly told – and the woman of the world will immediately understand – that when man sets his face against the proposal to bring in a hermaphroditic world, he does so because he can do his best work only in surroundings where he is perfectly free from suggestion and from restraint, and from the onus which all differential treatment imposes.

And I may add in connection with my own profession that when a rationalist man asks that he should not be the yoke-fellow of a 'rationalist' woman he does so also because he would wish to keep up as between men and women – even when they are philosophers – some of the modesty and reticence upon which our civilisation has been built up.

(d) Inextricably mixed up with the types which we have been discussing is the type of woman who is poisoned by her misplaced self-esteem; and who flies out at every man who does not pay homage to her intellect.

She is the woman who is affronted when a man avers that for him the glory of woman lies in her power of attraction, in her capacity for motherhood, and in unswerving allegiance to the ethics which are special to her sex.

I have heard such an intellectually embittered woman say, though she had been self-denyingly taken to wife, that "never in the whole course of her life had a man ever as much as done her a kindness."

The programme of this type of woman is, as a preliminary, to compel man to admit her claim to be his intellectual equal; and, that done, to compel him to divide up everything with her to the last penny, and so make her also his financial equal.

And her journals exhibit to us the kind of representative she desiderates. He humbly, hat in hand, asks for his orders from a batch of bitches standing legs akimbo.

(e) Following in the wake of these embittered human beings come troops of girls just grown up. All these will assure you, these young girls – and what is seething in their minds is stirring also in the minds in the girls in the colleges and schools which are staffed by unmarried feminists – that woman has suffered all manner of indignity and injustice at the hands of man.

And these young girls have been told about the intellectual, and moral, and financial value of woman – such tales as it never entered into the heart of man to conceive.

The programme of these young women is to be married upon their own terms. Man shall – so runs their scheme – work for their support – to that end giving up his freedom, and putting himself under orders, for many hours of the day; but they themselves must not be asked to give up any of their liberty to him, or to subordinate themselves to his interests, or to obey him in anything.

To obey a man would be to commit the unpardonable sin.

It is not necessary, in connection with a movement which proceeds on the lines set out above, any further to labour the point that there is in it an element of mental disorder. It is plain that it is there.

There is also a quite fatuous element in the programmes of the militant feminist. We have this element, for instance, in the doctrine that, notwithstanding the fact that the conditions of the labour market deny it to her, woman ought to receive the same wage as a man for the same work.

This doctrine is fatuous, because it leaves out of sight that, even if woman succeeds in doing the same work as man, he has behind him a much larger reserve of physical strength. As soon as a time of strain comes, a reserve of strength and freedom from periodic indisposition is worth paying extra for.

Fatuous also is the dogma that woman ought to have the same pay for the same work – fatuous because it leaves out of sight that woman's commercial value in many of the best fields of work is subject to a very heavy discount by reason of the fact that she cannot, like a male employee, work cheek by jowl with a male employer; nor work among men as a man with his fellow employees.

So much for the woman feminist's protest that she can conceive of no reason for a differential rate of pay for man.

Quite as fatuous are the marriage projects of the militant feminist. Every woman of the world could tell her – whispering it into her private ear – that if a sufficient number of men should come to the conclusion that it was not worth their while to marry except on the terms of fair give-and-take, the feminist woman's demands would have to come down.

It is not at all certain that the institution of matrimony – which, after all, is the great instrument in the levelling up of the financial situation of woman – can endure apart from some willing subordination on the part of the wife.

It will have been observed that there is in these programmes, in addition to the element of mental disorder and to the element of the fatuous, also a very ugly element of dishonesty. In reality the very kernel of the militant feminist movement is the element of immorality.

There is here not only immorality in the ends which are in view, but also in the methods adopted for the attainment of those ends. We may restrict ourselves to indicating wherein lies the immorality of the methods.

There is no one who does not discern that woman in her relations to physical force stands in quite a different position to man. Out of that different relation there must of necessity shape itself a special code of ethics for woman. And to violate that code must be for woman immorality.

So far as I have seen, no one in this controversy has laid his finger upon the essential point in the relations of woman to physical violence. It has been stated – and in the main quite truly stated – that woman in the mass cannot, like man, back up her beliefs by bringing physical force into play.

But the woman feminist here counters by insisting that she as an individual may have more physical force than an individual man. And it is quite certain – and it did not need feminist protests and 'pussy riots' to demonstrate it – that woman in the mass can bring a certain amount of physical force to bear.

The true inwardness of the relation in which woman stands to physical force lies not in the question of her having it at command, but in the fact that she cannot put it forth without placing herself within the jurisdiction of an ethical law.

The law against which she offends when she resorts to physical violence is not an ordinance of man; it is not written in the statutes of any state; it has not been enunciated by any human law-giver. It belongs to those unwritten, and unassailable, and irreversible commandments of religion which we suddenly and mysteriously become aware of when we see them violated.

The law which the militant feminist has violated is among the ordinances of that code which brands it as an ignominy when a man leaves his fellow in the lurch and saves his own life; and which makes it an outrage for a man to do violence to a woman. To violate any ordinance of that code is more dishonourable than to transgress every statutory law.

We see acknowledgment of it in the fact that even the uneducated man in the street resents it as an outrage to civilisation when he sees a man strike a blow at a woman. But to the man who is committing the outrage it is a thing simply unaccountable that any one should fly out at him.

In just such a case is the militant feminist. She cannot understand why any one should think civilisation is outraged when she scuffles in the street with a policeman. If she asks for an explanation, it perhaps behoves a man to supply it.

Up to the present in the whole civilised world there has ruled a truce of God as between man and woman. That truce is based upon the solemn covenant that within the frontiers of civilisation (outside them of course the rule lapses) the weapon of physical force may not be applied by man against woman; nor by woman against man.

Under this covenant, the reign of force which prevails in the world without comes to an end when a man enters his household. Under this covenant that half of the human race which most needs protection is raised up above the waves of violence. Within the terms of this compact everything that woman has received from man, and everything man receives from woman, is given as a free gift.

Again, under this covenant a full half of the programme of Western democracy has been realised; and a foundation has been laid upon which it may be possible to build higher; and perhaps finally in the ideal future to achieve the abolition of physical violence and war.

And it is this solemn covenant, the covenant so faithfully kept by man, which has been violated by the militant feminist in the interest of her morbid, stupid, ugly, and dishonest programmes.

Is it wonder if men feel that they have had enough of the militant feminist, and that society would be well rid of her if she were crushed under the shields of riot police?

We may turn now to that section of woman feminists – one is almost inclined to doubt whether it any longer exists – which is opposed to all violent measures, though it numbers in its ranks women who are stung to the quick by the thought that man, who will concede equality to the lowest and most degraded of his own sex, withholds it from her.

When that excited and somewhat pathetic appeal is addressed to us, we have only to consider what is really being withheld. When one realises that even the noblest woman would shrink from any personal exercise of violence, one would have thought that it would have come home to her that it is not precisely her job to engage with all the cold, hard practicalities of keeping a civilised society alive.

But the opportunist – the practical politician, as he calls himself – will perhaps here intervene, holding forth in some such language as this: "Granting all you say, granting, for the sake of argument, that the principle of giving equality to woman is unsound, and that evil must ultimately come of it, how can you get over the fact that no very conspicuous harm has resulted from gender equality in the countries which have adopted it? And can any firm reasons be rendered for the belief that the giving of equality to women in the UK would be any more harmful?"

A very few words will supply the answer.

The evils of feminism lie, first, in the fact that to give equality to women is to give it to a class who are quite incompetent to adjudicate upon political issues; secondly, in the fact that women are a class who cannot effectively back up their ideas by force; and, thirdly, in the fact that it may seriously embroil man and woman.

The first two aspects of the question have already in this controversy been adequately dealt with. There remains the last issue.

From the point of view of this issue the conditions which we have to deal with in this country are the absolute antithesis of those ruling in any of the countries and states which have adopted gender equality.

When feminism fully was embraced in these countries it was embraced in some for one reason, in others for another. In some it was adopted because it appealed to the doctrinaire politician as the proper logical outcome of a democratic and Socialistic policy. In others it was adopted because opportunist politicians saw in it an instrument by which they might gain electioneering advantages. So much was this the case that it sometimes happened that full equality was sprung upon a community which was quite unprepared and indifferent to it.

The cause of feminism was thus in the countries of which we speak neither in its inception nor in its realisation a question of revolt of woman against the oppression of man. It had, and has, no relation to the programmes of the militant feminists. By virtue of this, all the evils which spring from the embroiling of man and woman have in the countries in question been conspicuously absent.

Instead of seeing himself confronted by a section of embittered and hostile women which might at any time overthrow him, man there sees his women folk behaving practically everywhere in accordance with his directions, and lending him a hand to achieve his ends.

Whether or not this is for the good of the common weal is beside our present question. But it is clearly an arrangement which leads to amity and peace between a man and his womenkind, and through these to goodwill towards all women.

In the UK everything is different. If full equality is embraced here, it will have come as a surrender to a very violent feminist agitation – an agitation which we have traced back to our excess female population and the associated abnormal physiological conditions.

This is unquestionably the case in my own country, where the status of men is very much similar to – if not worse than – that given to prisoners of war in Vietnam, or even African slaves prior to the American Civil War. It is not going too far to say that the situation of gender "equality" in Sweden constitutes an ongoing humanitarian crisis, with good and decent men wrongly convicted of overblown sex charges, woman politicians riding roughshod over centuries of established tradition, and all with the blessing of so-called "normal" women in the populace.

If ever we concede full equality to woman in the UK, it will be accepted by the militant feminist, not as a truce, but as a victory which she will value only for the better carrying on of her fight against the oppression and injustice of man. A conciliation with hysterical revolt is neither an act of peace; nor will it bring peace.

Nor would the conferring of equality upon women carry with it any advantages from the point of view of finding a way out of the material entanglements in which woman is enmeshed, and thus ending the war between man and woman.

Peace will come again. It will come when woman ceases to believe and to teach all manner of evil of man despitefully. It will come when she ceases to impute to him as a crime her own natural disabilities, when she ceases to resent the fact that man cannot and does not wish to work side by side with her. And peace will return when every woman for whom there is no room in the UK seeks "rest" beyond the sea, "each one in the house of her husband," and when the woman who remains behind comes to recognise that she can, without sacrifice of dignity, give a willing subordination to the husband or father, who, when all is said and done, earns and lays up money for her.

5. Inconvenient fact: feminism is a route to anarchy

The feminist woman, when she is the kind of woman who piques herself upon her ethical impulses, will, even when she is intellectually very poorly equipped, and there is no imprint of altruism upon her life, assure you that nothing except the moral influence of woman, exerted through the legislation, which her practical mind would be capable of initiating, will ever avail to abate existing social evils, and to effect the moral redemption of the world.

It will not be amiss first to try to introduce a little clearness and order into our ideas upon those formidably difficult problems which the female SJW desires to attack, and then to consider how a rational reforming mind would go to work in the matter of proposing legislation for these.

First would come those evils which result from individuals seeking advantage to themselves by the direct infliction of injury upon others. Violations of the criminal law and the various forms of sweating and fleecing one's fellow-men come under this category.

Then would come the evils which arise out of purveying physiological and psychological refreshments and excitements, which are, according as they are indulged in temperately or intemperately, grateful and innocuous, or sources of disaster and ruin. The evils which are associated with the alcohol and gambling industries are typical examples.

Finally, there would come into consideration the evils of death or physical suffering deliberately inflicted by man upon man with a view to preventing worse evils. The evil of war would come under this category. In this same category might also come the much lesser evil of punitive measures inflicted upon criminals. And with this might be coupled the evil of killing and inflicting physical suffering upon animals for the advantage of man.

We may now consider how the rational reformer, as opposite to a rabid SJW, would in each case go to work.

He would not start with the assumption that it must be possible by some alteration of the law to abolish or conspicuously reduce any of the afore-mentioned evils; nor yet with the assumption that, if a particular alteration of the law would avail to bring about this result, that alteration ought necessarily to be made. He would recognise that many things which are theoretically desirable are unattainable; and that many legislative measures which could perfectly well be enforced would be barred by the fact that they would entail deplorable unintended consequences.

The rational legislator whom we have here in view would accordingly always take expert advice as to whether the desired object could be achieved by legal compulsion; and as to whether a projected law which satisfied the condition of being workable would give a balance of advantages over disadvantages.

In connection with a proposal for the prevention of sweating he would, for instance, take expert advice as to whether its provisions could be enforced; and whether, if enforceable, they would impose added hardships on any class of employees or penalties on any innocent class of employers.

In like manner in connection with a proposed modification in criminal procedure, the rational reformer would defer to the expert on the question as to whether such modification would secure greater certainty of punishment for the guilty without increasing the risk of convicting the innocent.

In connection with the second category of evils – the category under which would come those of drinking and betting – the rational legislative reformer would recognise the complete impracticability of abolishing by legislative prohibition physiological indulgences and the evils which sometimes attend upon them.

He would consider instead whether these attendant evils could be reduced by making the regulating laws more stringent; and whether more stringent restrictions – in addition to the fact that they would filch from the all too small stock of human happiness – would not, by paving the way for further invasions of personal liberty, cripple the free development of the community.

On the former question, which only experts could properly answer, the reasonable reformer would defer to their advice. The answer to the last question he would think out for himself.

In connection with the evils which are deliberately inflicted by man with a view to reaping either personal profit, or profit for the nation, or profit for humanity, the reasonable reformer would begin by making clear to himself that the world we live in is not such a world as idealism might conjure up, but a world of violence, in which life must be taken and physical suffering be inflicted.

And he would recognise that the vital material interests of the nation can be protected only by armed force; that civilisation can be safeguarded only by punishing violations of the criminal law; and that the taking of animal life and the infliction of a certain amount of physical suffering upon animals is essential to human well-being, comfort, and recreation; and essential also to the achievement of the knowledge which is required to combat disease.

It is vital to preserve a certain element of chaos in scientific research, to ensure that we keep encountering those 'happy accidents' by which we stumble on significant medical breakthroughs. Let us never forget that Pasteur and Fleming, although they were both excellent researchers in their respective fields, did not actually find cures for the diseases which they had sought to cure, but instead stumbled upon cures for totally unrelated diseases in the process.

Let us also preserve in our memories that ingenious British bacteriologist who, after theorising that microorganisms might be the vehicles of disease but not its cause, was pilloried cruelly by the ignorant mob of his day under the nickname "Sir Almost Wright".

Furthermore, on the subject of warfare, any reasonable reformer will direct his efforts not to the total abolition of war, but to the prevention of such wars as are not waged for really vital material interests, and to the abatement of the ferocities of warfare.

In the case of punishment for criminals he would similarly devote his efforts not to the abrogation of punishments, but to the relinquishment of any that are not reformatory, or really deterrent.

In like manner the reasonable reformer would not seek to prohibit the slaughtering of animals for food, or the killing off of animal pests, or the trapping, shooting, or hunting of animals for sport or profit, nor yet would he seek to prevent their utilisation of animals for the acquirement of knowledge.

He would direct his efforts to reducing the pain which is inflicted, and to preserving everywhere measure and scale – not sentimentally forbidding in connection with one form of utilisation of animals what is freely allowed in connection with another – but differentiating, if differentiating at all in favour of permitting the infliction of proportionately greater suffering in the case where national and humanitarian interests, than in the case where mere recreation and luxury and personal profit, are at stake.

Let it be noted that the man in the street makes no question about falling in with the fact that he is born into a world of violence, and he acquiesces in the principle that society, and, failing society, the individual, may employ force and take life in defence of vital material interests. And he frankly falls in with it being a matter of daily routine to kill and inflict suffering upon animals for human profit or advantage.

Even if these principles are not formulated by the man in the street in quite such plain terms, he not only carries them out in practice, but he conducts all his thinking upon these presuppositions.

He, for instance, would fall in with the proposition that morality does not require from man that he should give up taking life or inflicting physical suffering. And he would not cavil with the thinking that man should put reasonable limits to the amount of suffering he inflicts, and confine this within as narrow a range as possible – always requiring for the death or suffering inflicted some tangible advantage.

Moreover, if the question should be raised as to whether such advantage will result, the ordinary man will as a rule, where the matter lies beyond his personal ken, take expert opinion before intervening.

He will, for instance, be prepared to be so guided in connection with such questions as whether disease could, if more knowledge were available, be to a large extent prevented and cured; as to how far animal experiments would contribute to the acquirement of that knowledge; and as to how far the physical suffering which might be involved in these experiments can be minimised or abolished.

But not every man is prepared to fall in with this programme of inflicting physical suffering for the relief of physical suffering. There is also a type of spiritually-minded man who in this world of violence sets his face uncompromisingly against the taking of any life and the infliction of any physical suffering – refusing to make himself a partaker of evil.

An idealist of this type will, like Britain's Corbyn, be a pacifist. He will advocate a general pardon for criminals. He will be a vegetarian. He will not allow an animal's life to be taken in his house, though the mice scamper over his floors. And he will, consistently with his conviction that it is immoral to resort to force, refuse to take any part in legislation or government.

This attitude, which is that commended by the Hindu and the Buddhist religions, is, of course, a quite unpractical attitude towards life. It is, in fact, a self-destructive attitude, unless a man's fellow-citizens are prepared by forcible means to secure to him the enjoyment of the work of his hands or of his inherited property, or unless those who refuse to desist from the exercise of force are prepared to undertake the support of idealists.

I have now not seen my son Georg for more than a year. This is not due to my own negligence but that of his 'mother,' who has taken it upon herself to remove my presence from his life, and thus essentially castrate the boy in terms of his future development and incorporation of strong masculine role models. His balls have been removed, figuratively, by this woman – but will the state intervene?

I ask with only mild sarcasm; if she were to *literally* remove his physical balls (as I have sensed many times she wished to do), and rename the boy "Gerda," would the state intervene? Am I even allowed to ask the question? Will I have time added to my sentence for typing these words: "The Swedish state would not intervene to save a child from being physically castrated by his 'mother,' or any random passing woman"?

It is in the name of pacifism, idealism, feminism, social justice that my son has been stolen from me – and me from him. I will escape this place, Georg. I will save you.

To return to my point: we have not only these two classes of men – the ordinary man who has no compunction in resorting to force when the requirements of life demand it, and the idealist who refuses to have any lot or part in violence; there is also a hybrid. This male hybrid will descant on the general iniquity of violence, and then not only connive at those forms of violence which minister to his personal comforts, but also make a virtue of trying to abate by legal violence some particular form of physical suffering which happens to offend in a quite special manner his individual sensibility.

There is absolutely nothing to be said about this kind of reforming bullshitter, except only that anything which may be said in relation to the female SJW may be appositely said of him; and perhaps also this, that the ordinary man holds him both in intellectual and in moral contempt, and is resolved not to allow him to do any really serious injury to the community.

To become formidable this quasi-male person must, as he recognises, ally himself with the female SJW.

Passing on to deal with her, it imports us first to realise that while the ordinary man has – except where important constitutional issues were in question – been accustomed to leave actual legislation to the expert, the female SJW gives notice beforehand that she will insist on pressing forward her reforming schemes.

What would result from the ordinary voter legislating on matters which require expert knowledge will be plain to every one who will consider the evolution of law.

There stand over against each other here, as an example and a warning, the Roman Law, which was the creation of legal experts: the prætor and the jurisconsult; and the legal system of the Greeks, which was the creation of a popular assembly – and it was a popular assembly which was quite ideally intelligent.

Upon the Roman Law has been built the law of the greater part of the civilised world. The Greek is a by-word for inconsequence.

How can one, then, without cold shudders think of that legal system which the female amateur legal reformer would bring to the birth?

Let us consider her qualifications. Let us first take cognisance of the fact that the SJW will neither stand to the principle that man may, where this gives a balance of advantage, inflict on his fellow-man, and *a fortiori* upon animals, death and physical suffering; nor yet will she stand to the principle that it is ethically unlawful to do deeds of violence.

She spends her life halting between these two opinions, eternally pussyfooting.

She will, for instance, begin by announcing that it can never be lawful to do evil that good may come; and that killing and inflicting suffering is an evil. (In reality the precept of not doing evil that good may come has relation only to breaking for idealistic purposes moral laws of higher obligation.) She will then go back upon that and concede that war may sometimes be lawful, and that the punishment of criminals is not an evil. But if her emotions are touched by the forcible feeding of a criminal militant feminist, she will again go back upon that and declare that the application of force is an intolerable evil.

Or, again, she will concede that the slaughtering of animals for food is not an evil, but that what is really unforgivable is the infliction of physical suffering on animals. And all the time for her, as well as for man, calves and lambs are being emasculated to .make her meat succulent; wild animals are painfully done to death to provide her table with delicacies; birds with young in the nest are shot so that she may parade in their plumage; or fur-bearing animals are for her comfort and adornment massacred and tortured in traps.

When a male SJW who is co-responsible for these things begins to talk idealistic reforms, the ordinary decent man refuses to have anything more to say to him. But when a woman holds forth with this language, the man merely shrugs his shoulders. "It is," he tells himself, "after all, the woman whom God gave him."

It must be confessed that the problem as to how man with a dual nature may best accommodate himself to a world of violence presents a very difficult problem.

It would obviously be no solution to follow out everywhere a programme of violence. Not even the predatory animals do that. Tigers do not savage their cubs; hawks do not pluck hawks' eyes; and dogs do not fight their 'bitches'.

Nor would, as has been shown, the solution of the problem be arrived at by everywhere surrendering – if we had been given the grace to do this – to the urges of our animal natures.

What is required is to find the proper compromise. As to what that would be there is, as between the ordinary man and woman on the one side, and the male SJW and the battalions of sentimental women on the other, a conflict which is, to all intents and purposes, a sex war.

The compromise which ordinary human nature had fixed upon – and it is one which, ministering as it does to the survival of the race, has been adopted through the whole range of nature – is that of making within the world in which violence rules a series of enclaves in which the application of violence is progressively restricted and limited.

Outside the outermost of the series of ring fences thus constituted would be the realm of uncompromising violence such as exists when human life is endangered by wild animals, or murderous criminals, or savages. Just within this outermost fence would be civilised war – for in civilised war non-combatants and prisoners and wounded are excluded from the application of violence. In like manner we bring humanity in general within a more sheltered enclosure than animals – pet animals within a more sheltered enclosure than other animals. Again, we bring those who belong to the white race within a narrower protecting circle than mankind in general, and those of our own nation within a still narrower one.

Following out the same principle, we include women and children within a narrower shelter fence than our adult fellow-male; and we use the weapon of force more reluctantly when we are dealing with our relatives and friends than when we are dealing with those who are not personally known to us; and finally, we lay it aside more completely when we are dealing with the women of our households than when we are dealing with the males.

The cause of civilisation and of the amenities, and the welfare of the nation, of the family, and of woman, are all intimately bound up with a faithful adherence to this compromise.

But this policy imposes upon those whom it shelters from violence corresponding obligations.

In war non-combatants – not to speak of the wounded on the battlefield – must desist from hostile action on the pain of being shot down like wild beasts. And though an individual non-combatant might think it a patriotic action for him to take part in war, the thoughtful man would recognise that such action was a violation of a well-understood covenant made in the interest of civilisation, and that to break through this covenant was to abrogate a humanitarian arrangement by which the general body of non-combatants immensely benefits.

Exactly the same principle finds, as already pointed out, application when a woman employs direct violence, or aspires to exercise by voting indirect violence.

One always wonders if the feminist appreciates all that woman stands to lose and all that she imperils by resort to physical force. One ought not to have to tell her that, if she had to fight for her position, her status would be that which is assigned to her among the Muslims – not that which civilised man concedes to her.

From considering the compromise by which man adapts his dual nature to violence in the world, we turn to that which the female SJW would seek to impose by the aid of her protests.

Her proposal, as the reader will have discerned, would be that all those evils which make appeal to the feminine emotions should be legally prohibited, and that all those which fail to make this appeal shall be tolerated.

In the former class would be included those which come directly under woman's ken, or have been brought vividly before the eyes of her imagination by emotional description. And the specially intolerable evils will be those which, owing to the fact that they fall upon woman or her immediate belongings, induce in the female SJW pangs of sympathetic discomfort.

In the class of evils which the feminist is content to tolerate, or say nothing about, would be those which are incapable of evoking in her such sympathetic pangs, and she concerns herself very little with those evils which do not furnish her with a text for recriminations against man.

Conspicuous in this programme is the absence of any sense of proportion. One would have imagined that it would have been plain to everybody that the evils which individual women suffer at the hands of man are very far from being the most serious ills of humanity. One would have imagined that the suffering inflicted by disease and by bad social conditions – suffering which falls upon man and woman alike – deserved a first place in the thoughts of every reformer. And one might have expected it to be common knowledge that the wrongs individual men inflict upon women have a full counterpart in the wrongs which individual women inflict upon men. It may quite well be that there are mists which here "blot and fill the perspective" of the female SJW. But to look only upon one's own things, and not also upon the things of others, is not for that morally innocent.

There is further to be noted in connection with the female SJW that she has never been able to see why she should be required to put her aspirations into practical shape, or to consider ways and means, or to submit the practicability of her schemes to expert opinion. One also recognises that from a purely human point of view such tactics are judicious. For if the schemes of the female SJW were once to be reviewed from the point of view of their practicability, her utility as a legislator would come into question, and the feminist could no longer give out that there has been committed to her from on High a mission to draw water for mankind out of the wells of salvation.

Lastly, we have to reflect in connection with the female SJW that to go about proposing to reform the laws means to abandon that special field of usefulness which lies open to woman in alleviating misery and redressing those hard cases which will, under all laws and regulations of human manufacture and under all social dispositions, inevitably occur. Now when a woman leaves a social task which is commensurate with her abilities, and which asks from her personal effort and self-sacrifice, for a task which is quite beyond her abilities, but which, she thinks, will bring her personal kudos, shall we impute it to her for righteousness?

PART III – The Way Forward

1. The real feminist agenda

We have now sufficiently considered the feminist's humanitarian schemes, and we may lead up to the consideration of her further projects by contrasting feminism as it presents itself globally, with the kind of equality which is being agitated for in Western democracies.

In undeveloped countries generally where women are in a minority, and where owing to the fact that practically all have an opportunity of marrying, there are not for woman any difficult economic and physiological conditions, there is no woman's question; and by consequence no female SJW or feminist. The woman follows the lead of her menfolk. Under such conditions feminism leaves things as they are, except only that it undermines the logical foundations of the law, and still further debases the standard of public efficiency and public morality.

I trust that the skeptical reader will not harp on my lack of references and footnotes when making such assertions – which can be easily confirmed with even a rudimentary search. My resources at present are limited to a few minutes of restricted internet access a week, and an extremely unbalanced library (with a bizarrely thorough focus on early-20th century social sciences, and not a lot else).

In countries, such as the UK, where an excess female population has made economic difficulties for woman, and where the severe sexual restrictions, which here obtain, have bred in her sex-hostility, feminist activism has as its avowed ulterior object the abrogation of all distinctions which depend upon sex; and the achievement of the economic independence of woman.

To secure this economic independence every post, occupation, and Government service is to be thrown open to woman; she is to receive everywhere the same wages as man; male and female are to work side by side; and they are indiscriminately to be put in command the one over the other. The programme is, in fact, to give to woman an economic independence out of the earnings and taxes of man.

Nor does feminist ambition stop short here. It demands that women shall be included in every advisory committee, every governing board, every judicial bench, every electorate, every parliament, and every ministerial cabinet; further, that every masculine foundation, academy, trade union, scientific society and military unit shall be converted into a neutered institution – until we shall have everywhere one vast Punch and Judy show.

The proposal to bring man and woman together everywhere into extremely intimate relationships raises very grave questions. It brings up, first, the question of sexual complications; secondly, the question as to whether the tradition of modesty and reticence between the sexes is to be definitely sacrificed; and, most important of all, the question as to whether hermaphroditic conditions conditions would place obstacles in the way of intellectual work.

Of these issues the feminist puts the first two quite out of account. I have already elsewhere said my say upon these matters. With regard to the third, the feminist either fails to realise that purely intellectual intercourse – as distinguished from an intercommunion of mental images – with woman is to a large section of men repugnant; or else, perceiving this, she makes up her mind that, this notwithstanding, she will get her way by denouncing the man who does not welcome her as selfish; and by insisting that under feminism (the quotation is from Mill, the italics which question his sincerity are mine) "the mass of mental faculties available for the higher service of *man*kind would be doubled."

The matter cannot so lightly be disposed of. It will be necessary for us to find out whether really intimate association with woman on the purely intellectual plane is realisable. And if it is, in fact, unrealisable, it will be necessary to consider whether it is the exclusion of women from some masculine spheres; or the perpetual attempt of women to force their way into these, which would deserve to be characterised as selfish.

In connection with the former of these issues, we have to consider here not whether that form of intellectual cooperation in which the man plays the game, and the woman moves the pawns under his orders, is possible. That form of co-operation is of course possible, and it has, doubtless, certain utilities.

Nor yet have we to consider whether quite intimate and purely intellectual association on an equal footing between a particular man and a selected woman may or may not be possible. It will suffice to note that the feminist alleges that this also is possible; but everybody knows that the woman very often marries the man.

What we have to ask is whether – even if we leave out of regard the whole system of attractions or, as the case may be, repulsions which come into operation when the sexes are thrown together – purely intellectual intercourse between man and the typical unselected woman is not barred by the intellectual immoralities and limitations which appear to be secondary sexual characters of woman.

With regard to this issue, there would seem to be very little real difference of opinion among men. But there are great differences in the matter of candour. There are men who speak out, and who enunciate like Nietzsche that "man and woman are alien – never yet has any one conceived how alien."

There are men who, from motives of delicacy or policy, do not speak out – averse to saying anything that might be unflattering to woman.

And there are men who are by their profession of the feminist faith debarred from speaking out, but who upon occasion give themselves away.

Wherever we look we find aversion to compulsory intellectual co-operation with woman. We see it in the sullen attitude which the ordinary male student takes up towards the presence of women students in his classes. Practically every man feels that there is in woman – patent, or hidden away – an element of unreason which, when you come upon it, summarily puts an end to purely intellectual intercourse. One may reflect, for example, upon the way the feminism controversy has been conducted.

Proceeding now on the assumption that these things are so, and that man feels that he and woman belong to different intellectual castes, we come now to the question as to whether it is man who is selfish when he excludes women from his institutions, or woman when she unceasingly importunes for admittance. And we may define as selfish all such conduct as pursues the advantage of the agent at the cost of the happiness and welfare of the general body of mankind.

We shall be in a better position to pronounce judgment on this question of ethics when we have considered the following series of analogies:

When a group of earnest and devout believers meet together for special intercession and worship, we do not tax them with selfishness if they exclude unbelievers.

Nor do we call people who are really devoted to music selfish if, coming together for this, they make a special point of excluding the unmusical.

Nor again would the imputation of selfishness lie against members of a club for banning a candidate who would, they feel, be uncongenial.

Nor should we regard it as an act of selfishness if the members of a family circle, or of the same nation, or of any social circle, desired to come together quite by themselves.

Nor yet would the term selfish apply to a Goth club audience when they eject any one who belongs to a different social class to themselves and wears good clothes.

And the like would hold true of employees resenting their employers intruding upon them in their hours of leisure or entertainments If we do not characterise such exclusions as selfish, but rather respect and sympathise with them, it is because we recognise that the whole object and raison d'être of association would in each case be nullified by the weak-minded admission of the incompatible intruder.

We recognise that if any charge of selfishness would lie, it would lie against that intruder.

Now if this holds in the case where the interests of religious worship or music, or family, national, or social life, or recreation and relaxation after labour are in question, it will hold true even more emphatically where the interests of intellectual work are involved.

But the feminist will want to argue. She will – taking it as always for granted that woman has a right to all that men's hands or brains have fashioned – argue that it is very important for the intellectual development of woman that she should have exactly the same opportunities as man. And she will, scouting the idea of any differences between the intelligences of man and woman, discourse to you of their intimate affinity.

It will, perhaps, be well to clear up these points.

The importance of the higher development of woman is unquestionable.

But after all it is the intellect of man which really comes into account in connection with "the mass of mental faculties available for the higher service of mankind."

The maintenance of the conditions which allow of man's doing his best intellectual work is therefore an interest which is superior to that of the intellectual development of woman. And woman might quite properly be referred for her intellectual development to instructional institutions which should be special to herself.

Coming to the question of the intimate resemblances between the masculine and the feminine intelligence, no man would be venturesome enough to dispute these, but he may be pardoned if he thinks – one would hope in no spirit of exaltation – also of the differences.

We have an instructive analogy in connection with the learned societies.

It is uncontrovertible that every candidate for election into such a society will have, and will feel that he has, affinities with the members of that association. And he is invited to set these forth in his application. But there may also be differences of which he is not sensible. On that question the electors are the judges; and they are the final court of appeal.

There would seem to be here a moral which the feminist would do well to lay to heart. There is also another lesson which she might very profitably consider. A quite small difference will often constitute as effective a bar to a useful and congenial co-operation as a more fundamental difference.

In the case of a body of intellectual workers one might at first sight suppose that so small a distinction as that of belonging to a different nationality – sex, of course, is an infinitely profounder difference – would not be a bar to unrestricted intellectual co-operation.

But in point of fact it is in every country, in every learned society, a uniform rule that when foreign scientists or scholars are admitted they are placed not on the ordinary list of working members, but on a special list.

One discerns that there is justification for this in the fact that a foreigner would in certain eventualities be an incompatible person.

One may think of the eventuality of the learned society deciding to recognise a national service, or to take part in a national movement. And one is not sure that a foreigner might not be an incompatible person in the eventuality of a scientist or scholar belonging to a nationality with which the foreigner's country was at feud being brought forward for election. And he would, of course, be an impossible person in a society if he were, in a spirit of chauvinism, to press for a larger representation of his own fellow-countrymen.

Now this is precisely the kind of way man feels about woman. He recognises that she is by virtue of her sex for certain purposes an incompatible person; and that, quite apart from this, her secondary sexual characters might in certain eventualities make her an impossible person.

We may note, before passing on, that these considerations would seem to prescribe that woman should be admitted to masculine institutions only when real humanitarian grounds demand it; that she should – following here the analogy of what is done in the learned societies with respect to foreigners – be invited to co-operate with men only when she is quite specially eminent, or beyond all question useful for the particular purpose in hand; and lastly, that when co-opted into any masculine institution woman should always be placed upon a special list, to show that it was proposed to confine her co-operation within certain specified limits.

From these general questions, which affect only the woman with intellectual aspirations, we pass to consider what would be the effect of feminism upon the rank and file of women if it made of these co-partners with man in work. They would suffer not only because woman's physiological disabilities and the restrictions which arise out of her sex place her at a great disadvantage when she has to enter into competition with man, but also because under feminism man would be less and less disposed to take off woman's shoulders a part of her burden.

And there can be no dispute that the most valuable financial asset of the ordinary woman is the possibility that a man may be willing – and may, if only woman is disposed to fulfil her part of the bargain, be not only willing but anxious – to support her and to secure for her, if he can, a measure of that freedom which comes from the possession of money.

In view of this every one who has a real fellow-feeling for woman, and who is concerned for her material welfare, as a father is concerned for his daughter's, will above everything else desire to nurture and encourage in man the sentiment of chivalry, and in woman that disposition of mind that makes chivalry possible.

A personal note. In many ways, I am glad my retard sister did not live to see her 18th birthday. Despite having all the love in the world for the poor creature, I know in my heart that she would never have been able to inspire in the heart of any man (except, perhaps, for the most twisted and irredeemable form of pervert) anything like the natural, wholesome passion which drives men to serve and protect all normal women. I think now, as I used to think before her accident, that it is perhaps kinder for such unfortunates to be spared the pain of coming up against their own innate inferiority; and the world's cruel but evolutionarily justified indifference to their suffering.

The woman workers who have to fight the battle of life for themselves would indirectly profit from a widespread fostering of chivalry; for those women who are supported by men do not compete in the limited labour market which is open to the woman worker.

From every point of view, therefore, except perhaps that of the exceptional woman who would be able to hold her own against masculine competition – and men always issue informal letters of naturalisation to such an exceptional woman – feminism would be a social disaster.

2. The time is now

Is there then, let us ask ourselves, if feminist activism with its programme of full equality is barred as leading to social disaster, any palliative or corrective that can be applied to the present discontents of woman?

If such is to be found, it is to be found only by placing clearly before us the feminist's grievances.

These grievances are, first, the difficulties of the woman who seeks to earn her living by work other than unskilled menial labour; secondly, the difficult physiological conditions in which woman is placed by the excess of the female over the male population and by her diminished chances of marriage; and thirdly, the tedium which obsesses the life of the woman who is not forced, and cannot force herself, to work. On the top of these grievances comes the fact that the feminist conceives herself to be harshly and unfairly treated by man. This last is the fire which sets a light to all the inflammable material.

It would be quite out of question to discuss here the economic and physiological difficulties of woman. Only this may be said: it is impossible, in view of the procession of starved and frustrated lives which is continuously filing past, to close one's eyes to the urgency of this woman's problem.

After all, the primary object of all civilisation is to provide for every member of the community food and shelter and fulfilment of natural cravings. And when, in what passes as a civilised community, a whole class is called upon to go without any one of these our human requirements, it is little wonder that it should break out.

But when a way of escape stands open revolt is not morally justified.

Thus, for example, a man who is born into, but cannot support himself in, a superior class of society is not, as long as he can find a livelihood abroad in a humbler walk in life, entitled to revolt.

No more is the woman who is in economic or physiological difficulties. For, if only she has the pluck to take it, a way of escape stands open to her.

She can emigrate; she can go out from the social class in which she is not self-supporting into a humbler social class in which she could earn a living; and she can forsake conditions in which she must remain a spinster for conditions in which she may perhaps become a mother. Only in this way can the problem of finding work, and relief of tedium, for the woman who now goes idle be resolved.

If women were to avail themselves of these ways of escape out of unphysiological conditions, the woman agitator would probably find it as difficult to keep alive a passionate agitation for feminist as the Islamist hate preacher to keep alive a passionate agitation for the imposition of Sharia law.

For the happy wife and mother is never passionately concerned about feminist activism. It is always the woman who is galled either by physiological hardships, or by the fact that she has not the same amount of money as man, or by the fact that man does not desire her as a co-partner in work, and withholds the homage which she thinks he ought to pay to her intellect.

For this class of grievances the present education of woman is responsible. The girl who is growing up to woman's estate is never taught where she stands relatively to man. She is not taught anything about woman's physical disabilities. She is not told – she is left to discover it for herself when too late – that child and husband are to woman physiological requirements. She is not taught the defects and limitations of the feminine mind. One might almost think there were no such defects and limitations; and that woman was not always overestimating her intellectual power. And the ordinary girl is not made to realise woman's intrinsically inferior money-earning capacity. She is not made to realise that the woman who cannot work with her hands is generally hard put to earn enough to keep herself alive in the incomplete condition of a spinster.

As a result of such education, when, influenced by the feminist movement, woman comes to institute a comparison between herself and man, she brings into that comparison all those qualities in which she is substantially his equal, and leaves out of account all those in which she is his inferior.

The failure to recognise that man is the master, and why he is the master, lies at the root of feminist activism movement. By disregarding man's superior physical force, the power of compulsion upon which all government is based is disregarded. By leaving out of account those powers of the mind in which man is the superior, woman falls into the error of thinking that she can really compete with him, and that she belongs to the self-same intellectual caste. Finally, by putting out of sight man's superior money-earning capacity, the power of the purse is ignored.

Uninstructed woman commits also another fundamental error in her comparison. Instead of comparing together the average man and the average woman, she sets herself to establish that there is no defect in woman which cannot be discovered also in man; and that there is no virtue or power in the ordinary man which cannot be discovered also in woman. Which having been established to her satisfaction, she is led inevitably to the conclusion that there is nothing whatever to choose between the sexes. And from this there is only a step to the position that human beings ought to be assigned, without distinction of sex, to each and every function which would come within the range of their individual capacities, instead of being assigned as they are at present: men to one function, and women to another.

Here again women ought to have been safeguarded by education. She ought to have been taught that even when an individual woman comes up to the average of man this does not abrogate the disqualification which attaches to a difference of sex. Nor yet – as every one who recognises that we live in a world which conducts itself by generalisations will see – does it abrogate the disqualification of belonging to an inferior intellectual caste.

The present system of feminine education is blameworthy not only in the respect that it fails to draw attention to these disqualifications and to teach woman where she stands; it is even more blameworthy in that it fails to convey to the girl who is growing up any conception of that absolutely elementary form of developmental morality which consists in distinguishing 'me' from 'you'.

Instead of her educators encouraging every girl to assert "rights" as against man, and put forward claims, they ought to teach her with respect to him those lessons of behaviour which are driven home once for all into every boy at a public school.

Just as there you learn that you may not make unwarranted demands upon your fellow, and just as in the larger world every nation has got to learn that it cannot with impunity lay claim to the possessions of its neighbours, so woman will have to learn that when things are not offered to her, and she has not the power to take them by force, she has got to make the best of things as they are. One would wish for every girl who is growing up to womanhood that it might be brought home to her by some refined and ethically-minded member of her own sex how insufferable a person woman becomes when, like a spoilt child, she exploits the indulgence of man; when she proclaims that it is his duty to serve her and to share with her his power and possessions; when she makes an outcry when he refuses to part with what is his own; and when she insists upon thrusting her society upon men everywhere.

And every girl ought to be warned that to embark upon a policy of recrimination when you do not get what you want, and to proclaim yourself a martyr when, having hit, you are hit back, is the way to get yourself thoroughly disliked.

Finally, every girl ought to be shown, in the example of the militant feminist, how revolt and martyrdom, undertaken in order to possess oneself of what belongs to others, effects the complete disorganisation of moral character.

No one would wish that in the education of girls these quite unlovely things should be insisted upon more than was absolutely necessary. But one would wish that the educators of the rising generation of women should, basing themselves upon these foundations, point out to every girl how great is woman's debt to civilisation; in other words, how much is under civilisation done for woman by man.

And one would wish that, in a world which is rendered unwholesome by feminism, every girl's eyes were opened to comprehend the great outstanding fact of the world: the fact that, turn where you will, you find individual man showering upon individual woman – one man in tribute to her enchantment, another out of a sense of gratitude, and another just because she is something that is his – every good thing which, equality or no equality, she never could have procured for herself.

Afterword

I am Elias Lundgren. I am still 34 years old (just about). I am still a man. I still have a cock and balls between my legs – thank Odin. Do these facts still make me a criminal? I'll let you be the judge now, dear reader.

My ex-wife visited me this week. She did not bring Georg, as I have asked – begged – her to do for months now. She told me that if I keep writing to her, she will take out a restraining order.

A restraining order against a man already in prison. Can there be a more perfect metaphor for the situation facing the male in modern society? We are forced into social and intellectual castration, by women who are terrified of our true potential, and seek to de-level the playing field at every opportunity.

I did not reply, after she said that. I sat and stared at her, wondering quietly whether to slam my fist against the glass. Eventually she stopped talking, said quietly that she forgave me, and got up to leave.

"Sara," I said in a commanding tone. She turned around – and, despite what I'm sure she has told her friends, she was the only one crying. I looked her dead in the eyes, not rising from my seat.

"Georg is my son, and only mine. I will reclaim him when my trials are ended, and I escape this place. You will not keep him from me. These are the last words I will ever waste on you. Go to Hell, you goddamned frigid bitch."

My heart roared like an erupting volcano as I said those words, so long nurtured. I could see then that she was a broken woman, and she sobbed as she left that place. I did not weep; I have no tears left to cry over that waste of skin.

I have returned to my cell now, but I do not think any man has eve felt so free in his life.

My name is Elias Lundgren. I am not ashamed.

I have balls. And I intend to use them.